Magic Licking Lollipops

Lynn and Lily love licking lollipops, and lollies of all colours, shapes and sizes. But this time, have they bitten off more than they can chew?

This picture book targets the /l/ sound and is part of *Speech Bubbles 2*, a series of picture books that target specific speech sounds within the story.

The series can be used for children receiving speech therapy, for children who have a speech sound delay/disorder, or simply as an activity for children's speech sound development and/or phonological awareness. They are ideal for use by parents, teachers or caregivers.

Bright pictures and a fun story create an engaging activity perfect for sound awareness.

Picture books are sold individually, or in a pack. There are currently two packs available – *Speech Bubbles 1* and *Speech Bubbles 2.* Please see further titles in the series for stories targeting other speech sounds.

Melissa Palmer is a Speech Language Therapist. She worked for the Ministry of Education, Special Education in New Zealand from 2008 to 2013, with children aged primarily between 2 and 8 years of age. She also completed a diploma in children's writing in 2009, studying under author Janice Marriott, through the New Zealand Business Institute. Melissa has a passion for articulation and phonology, as well as writing and art, and has combined these two loves to create *Speech Bubbles*.

What's in the pack?

User Guide

Vinnie the Dove

Rick's Carrot

Harry the Hopper

Have You Ever Met a Yeti?

Zack the Buzzy Bee

Asher the Thresher Shark

Catch That Chicken!

Will the Wolf

Magic Licking Lollipops

Jasper the Badger

Platypus and Fly

The Dragon Drawing War

Magic Licking Lollipops

Lollipops

Targeting the /l/ Sound

Melissa Palmer

Routledge
Taylor & Francis Group

LONDON AND NEW YORK

First published 2021
by Routledge
2 Park Square, Milton Park, Abingdon, Oxon OX14 4RN

and by Routledge
52 Vanderbilt Avenue, New York, NY 10017

Routledge is an imprint of the Taylor & Francis Group, an informa business

British Library Cataloguing-in-Publication Data
A catalogue record for this book is available from the British Library

Library of Congress Cataloging-in-Publication Data
A catalog record has been requested for this book

ISBN: 978-1-138-59784-6 (set)
ISBN: 978-0-367-64883-1 (pbk)
ISBN: 978-1-003-12675-1 (ebk)

Typeset in Calibri
by Newgen Publishing UK

Magic Licking Lollipops

Lynn loved to lick lollipops. She liked the flavour and the way they looked.

Lily loved to lick lollipops too. She liked how they would roll on her tongue.

Lynn and Lily found a little lolly shop down a long path.

The sign on the door said 'Alan's Magic Lollies'.

"**L**et's go have a **l**ook," said **Li**ly.

The **litt**le girls went down the **l**ong path. What would be inside?

The shop was full of lollies!

Long ones, short ones, little ones, big ones! Pink lollies, green lollies, blue and yellow lollies. Some were striped, some spotted. Some had coloured swirls all over.

"Welcome to my **lo<u>ll</u>y** shop! What wi<u>ll</u> you choose?" asked A<u>l</u>an, the **lo<u>ll</u>y** shop keeper.

Lynn and Lily bought lots of lollies – blue, yellow, pink, striped and spotted.

They licked some yellow lollipops. A funny thing began to happen.

"**Li**ly! Your face is ye**ll**ow **l**ike your **lo**l**l**ipop!" said **L**ynn.

"You too!" said **Li**ly.

They laughed and laughed. They licked more lollipops
-l-l-l-l-l-l-l-l-l-l-l-l-l-l-

Their faces turned pink, their faces turned blue.

Their faces were striped and spotted too!

Soon, the **loll**ipops were a**ll** gone. "We can't go home **l**ooking **l**ike this! What wi**ll** we do?" said **L**ynn.

"Eat these; you'll be good as new." Alan gave them lollipops clear like glass. "They will take the colours all away."

Lily and Lynn licked the lollipops as quickly as they could.
-l-l-l-l-l-l-l-l-l-l-l- lick!

Slowly their faces turned back to normal.

Lily and Lynn went home, swinging their legs and singing of the magic licking lollipops that make you change colour.

What fun!